A Circle of Stones

Journeys & Meditations for Modern Celts

Erynn Rowan Laurie

ISBN 1-57353-106-5

Second Printing 1998

EPB-AW-106
an
ESCHATON BOOK
from

ESCHATON
P R O D U C T I O N S , I N C .
60 East Chestnut Street, #236
Chicago, IL 60611-2012

Send an S.A.S.E. for our current catalog!

Visit Eschaton on the Web:
http://www.eschatonbooks.com

Contents

Foreword

Three candles that illumine every darkness:
truth, nature, knowledge
from the Irish Triads

The ancient Celts were a people immersed in poetry. Their written records tell us that the most highly respected people in society were poets and story tellers, those who kept alive the fire of tradition. Poetry was history, genealogy, praise and damnation. In a way, poetry was the magic of creation itself, bringing into being the great heroes, the acts of the deities and the memory of the people. The *Senchus Mor*, or the Great Ancient Laws of the Irish say that "the preserving shrine is nature and what is preserved in it," and that all things are "connected by a thread of poetry."

In the modern world, we have lost this deep poetic passion, this connecting thread. Our link with myth and nature's preserving shrine has been shattered; our lives follow the rapid rhythm of machines and not liquid bird song or the blowing of wind through scented trees. Still, some people attempt to break free from the tyranny of scientific materialism that dis-spirits and de-sacralizes the natural world.

Modern Paganism's varied traditions have rites to celebrate the turning of the seasons, rituals for marking the passages of human life, and celebrations of the waxing and waning of the moon. We seek to reconnect with the rhythms of our ancestors, to touch and share their experience of the sacred through acknowledging the movement of time in its cycles. In small, individual acts of courage, we attempt to re-weave the fabric of our poetic connections with nature.

Many spiritual traditions recommend meditations upon rising, before the activity of the day begins, and again in the evening, as a reflection upon the day's accomplishments. Within this book are poems drawn from Celtic oral and literary tradition, accompanied by modern affirmations, meditations and activities. They are arranged as a circle of stones, a sacred space that we can enter in the morning and after our day's work is done, or any time that we need to pause and remember the power of poetry to calm or excite the soul.

Within the circle, ways of journeying into the three realms of land, sea and sky are taught. These are powerful tools for seeking wisdom and developing and deepening our connection with the earth. The techniques take time, as do all worthwhile things. No promises of instant success or enlightenment are made. The most significant accomplishment within the circle lies in contemplative repetition, using its gentle rhythm to reach a peaceful state of consciousness for sorting through the cares of the day and affirming that tomorrow our work can be done in greater harmony with the world around us.

We cannot go back in time to ask the ancient Celts how they practiced their religions, meditated, or travelled into the Otherworlds. Their religious traditions did not survive intact into this century, much as we might desire to learn their secrets. Because of this, what is presented here can only be a partial reconstruction and an extrapolation based on best guesses and existing source material. It is not, and cannot be an ancient path. Like all other modern Pagan traditions, it is a creation of our time and place, for modern practitioners. This circle of stones was birthed with the hope that it preserves something of the feel of early Celtic religion, bringing those concepts forward in a manner suitable for modern times and modern people. It is an attempt to find the connecting thread of poetry.

As with any act of creation, this book would not have been possible without several things. First, there has been the inspiration of friends. There is also the deeply appreciated support and encouragement of my husband over the four years it has taken to compile the right poetic pieces and to set concepts on paper. Many people have given generously of their time and effort as I have shamelessly cloistered myself; ransacking libraries, spending entire nights in front of the phosphor screen, refusing to eat because I had to type "just one more page." The work of a writer is not one of moderation.*

My thanks go to Moondancer, Raven and Zanoni for the original idea of a meditation circle; to Helen and Manya, who understand me when I'm possessed by the spirit of writing and take me out to eat when I've been at it too long; to Bjoern, who typed in the manuscript; to my online friends who have been behind me all the way, especially John G., who had enough faith in the work to take it to a publisher; and to Brendan at Eschaton, for taking a chance on an unknown author. Most of all my love to Gordon for his infinite patience, fervent faith and deep dedication, without whom none of this would have been possible.

Erynn Rowan Laurie
Seattle, 1994

* The illustrations in this book are by the often-used by rarely credited George Bain, beloved of Celtophiles everywhere.

Walking
the
Cosmic
Circle

Celtic myth is encompassed by stone. Ancient sacred circles stand in the midst of the landscape, and their presence is imprinted on Celtic consciousness. The passage of seasons and years was measured by carefully laid stone, built by mysterious people who predated the Celts. Stones mark sacred sites; hilltops, wells, graves and royal plains. The great hero Cu Chulainn died tied to a standing stone, so that he could leave this life standing on his feet.

The stones which have been most strongly impressed upon us are the circles, images of the sacred circle of life and death, the womb of the Goddess, the sun and moon. Circles reflect a cyclic understanding of time and the cosmos. Located in places of power, some circles are approached by avenues of standing stones, the paths through which ritual and energy flow.

The sacred cosmology of the ancient Celts has been lost to the ravages of time and change. All that remains are hints to be sifted from tales, poetry, and fragmentary traditions. Understanding this limitation, a working model for modern ritual and meditation can be proposed. What follows is a reconstruction, based upon many years of tracing the threads of myth, image and poetry.

The basis of our circle is the great triskele or triple spiral; the three realms of land, sea and sky. Beneath us, firm and solid, lies the land. It supports and feeds us. Surrounding this is the sea, the boundary between our world and the realms of the Gods. Above all arches the sky. It is upon this division, rather than the traditional western four elements of earth, air, fire and water, that the ancient Celts based their concept of the universe. Oaths were sworn by land, sea and sky. All things lived within the circle.

Connecting these realms, and flowing within them, is fire. Fire is the symbol of the presence of the Gods, spiritual energy, and the power of the land and the *tuath* or tribe. It is the connection between humanity and the Gods. In the language of Celtic myth, fire is the nature of poetry, of inspiration itself. It is the thread which connects all things. This fire is called *imbas*, "poetic inspiration." The Irish poet Aimirgen alluded to imbas when he spoke of "a god who shapes fire for a head."

3

Time was separated into light and darkness, summer and winter. Day began with the fall of night, and holy day celebrations thus began the night before, as the November festival of Samhain begins on the last night of October. Likewise, the year began with Samhain, or "summer's end."

Both Ireland and Wales were divided into geographical provinces surrounding a sacred center. These provinces corresponded roughly to the four directions, leading to a five-fold categorization of space.

This division into five areas is emphasized in Irish myth. Fintan, who lived many lifetimes in a number of shapes, knew all the history of the island. He divided the island in this way: "knowledge in the west, battle in the north, prosperity in the east, music in the south, kingship in the centre."[1] A simpler division gives us the four winds, which we find in many folk tales and poems.

From the north, along with battle, came the four treasures of the Tuatha de Danann, the ancient Gods of Ireland. Before their arrival in Ireland, they stayed in four cities "in the northern islands of the world, learning druidry and knowledge and prophecy and magic, till they were expert in the arts of pagan cunning."[2] In each city they learned new magic and were given a different object. From Falias they brought the Stone of Fal. Gorias was the source of the Spear of Lugh. The Sword of Nuada came from Findias, and the Cauldron of Daghda was given to them in Murias. The treasures are the precursors of the grail hallows. There is no evidence that they were elemental or directional tools of earth, air, fire and water, although some people use them in this way.

In the center of our cosmic circle lies the well of wisdom. It is surrounded by a grove of nine hazel trees. Beside the well is the world tree, the embodiment of the ancient ancestral deity known as Bile [bee-lah]. His name means "a sacred tree." Circling above the tree, rotating through its branches, is the region of the summer stars which was spoken of by the Welsh bard Taliesin.

Nine is a deeply significant number in Celtic mythology. Some scholars suggest that the early Celtic week was nine days

4

long. Ritual actions are often shown as taking nine days to perform. There is some evidence that the Celts had nine *duile* or "elements." The list varied according to time and place, but a sample group might include earth, stone, salt, water, rain, cloud, sun, stars and wind. These duile do not appear to be much like the elements of western magic. It is doubtful that they were ever used in the same way.

Ruling the cosmic triskele are the great deities Danu, Manannan and Bile. All three appear to be pre- or pan-Celtic, and have long and venerable histories.

Danu [*dah*-noo] is the Mother of the Gods. She represents the land from which the de Danann came. This land is not a physical place, but is instead the sacred geography of the Otherworld realms. Danu is the principle of birth and beginnings, of generation and of fertility. She is the hidden source of the Well of Segais, which is the abode of the Salmon of Wisdom. In continental Europe, she is the Goddess of springs, giving her name to dozens of rivers such as the Danube and the Don. Although there are no positively identified images of Danu in Irish iconography, the sheila-na-gig seems quite appropriate.

Manannan [*man*-ah-nawn] holds the keys to the Otherworld realms. He was a king of the de Danann, and gave them access to the sidhe mounds. Some sources claim that he was kin to the Tuatha de Danann, but others claim he is far older. His sacred island in the physical world is Inis Mann, the Isle of Man. It is my belief that he is one of the primordial Gods of Celtic creation. He is Lord of Tir fo Thuinn, the Land Under Sea and of Tir na mBan, the Isle of Women, as well as having many other, very significant roles. Water is a boundary between the worlds, and Manannan directs the *imramma* voyages. He symbolizes the transition from one world to another. His personal symbol is known to be the triskele.

Bile is in some sources the husband of Danu. He is the ruler of the realm of the dead, Lord of Death. As Lord of the Dead, he is the agency through which we may contact the ancestors, and vice versa. He was said to be one of the early ancestors of the Milesians, dwelling in central Europe. On the continent, he was known as Belenos. Gaulish iconography links him with solar symbols and stags. He rules the cycles of time and the seasons. His image is more commonly known as "Cernunnos."

Each of these components is a piece of the Celtic worldview. They can be represented as a circle of meditative beads, divided in various ways. You can create your own circle following the instructions in the next chapter.

The first part of our circle is the Gate of Divine Mysteries. It is a pendant which dangles from the body of the circlet, linked to it by the three beads of the Inner Flame. The Gate of Divine Mysteries stands for many things. It is the hidden source of Well of Wisdom, the triskele of Manannan, the threefold eponymous Goddesses of Ireland -- Fodhla, Banbha and Eriu. It may stand for any triplicity revered by the Celts, and it is the source of all creation. One side of the pendant may be marked with a triskele.

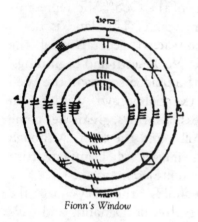

Fionn's Window

The other may hold the symbol called Fionn's Window, an Ogham wheel found in the 14th century CE *Book of Ballymote*. This can be used as mirror, gateway and cosmological mandala.

The Inner Flame represents that spark within us that is our link with the Gods. It is the internal energy of the World Tree, or the central pillar of the sky which reaches beyond that canopy into the realms beyond human understanding. It is the Maypole, the centerpost, and the watchfire which guides us on our journeys, and which sees us safely back again. It is the sacred inspiration of poetry. The Inner Flame symbolizes also the three cauldrons of meditation, which the Irish poets discuss in a poem called "The Cauldron of Poesy." It is the ritual processional that leads us into the body of the circle.

These beads are connected to the main body of the circle at a significant point. It is called Double Spiral Gate. This bead can be seen as the Gate of Winter and Summer, of Samhain and Beltain, the Gate of Night and Day, or the Gate of Birth and Death. All of these are equivalent concepts in the cycle of day, year, and lifetime. It encompasses all the dualistic opposites, and implies a hidden third part, as graphically presented in the Lindisfarne spiral. This is the place where Manannan stands as the key, the gate, and the

Lindisfarne Double Spiral

gatekeeper between Danu and Bile, life and death. It is the physical manifestation of the Well of Wisdom where we may drink the water and sit on its banks. The Double Spiral Gate may also be represented as the hole in the stone, another symbolic gateway.

The Double Spiral Gate rests between the north and west winds. In the Irish tales, magic has its source in the north of the world, but it arrives in the west, and so our point of origin for physical manifestation in the circle is located in the "northwest quadrant." Our arrival is also placed here because it is between Land and Sea, the symbolic meeting place of all three realms.

From this Gate, we move to the left, and upward along the circle to the bead which signifies Danu. Danu and Bile are the essence of life and death, guardians of the realms beyond life, and of the land of the dead. They are the boundary all of created reality and define time and the cycle of seasons. They, with Manannan, define, guard, and grant access to all the realms of manifest and unmanifest reality. These three are our guides to the Otherworld realms and at the same time are themselves embodiments of these realms.

After this is the bead of the Treasure of Falias, Lia Fail [lee-ah fohl], which is surrounded by beads signifying the four winds. Its Guardian is Morfessa, which means "great knowledge/wisdom". This Treasure represents the mythic essence of the sacred land, and is the solid support of the Tree of Life, or the centerpost which reaches beyond the sky. It was the standing stone which cried out for the High Kings of Ireland confirming their acceptance by the land's Sovereignty, and it stood on the hill of Tara, the mystical and sacred center of Ireland.

Next are nine beads symbolizing the Sacred Land. These nine beads represent the physical world as an island in the surrounding sea. In ancient times, many cultures viewed the known world as an island, and this viewpoint is not unique to the Celts. For the Irish, in fact, the world was an island surrounded by ocean, and come to only by crossing that formidable barrier. The land was named for the three Goddesses Fodla, Banbha and Eriu by Aimirgen during the course of its conquest by the Sons of Mil, ancestors of the human Gaels.

We come next to the Treasure of Gorias, the Spear of Lugh, and surrounding beads for the four winds. Its Guardian is Esras. This Treasure is the magical spear which is symbolic of the world tree, the link between earth and sky. Lugh is the many-skilled God who is capable in all the arts and sciences. The spear itself can also link earth and sky when it is thrown from the hand of the warrior. It is a symbol of protection from harm, of willingness to stand firm in the face of troubles, and of the cohesion of the people as a social, spiritual and political unit.

This leads into the nine beads of the Endless Sky. It is the canopy above land and sea. The sky tells the passing of days and seasons, and the seasons of one's life. By observing its cycles we can come to know the mysteries of time, of planting and the movement of herds, of augury by the motion of clouds and the movement and sounds of birds. The sky is everpresent above us, and it is the realm of the winds and of rain, sunlight, and snow.

Next is the Treasure of Finias, the Sword of Nuadha and its four winds. Its Guardian is Uscias. This Treasure represents the divisions of society and between the realms of this world and the Otherworlds. It is the weapon of Nuadha, the King who was wounded and removed from power due to his imperfection. His wounded arm was replaced by one of silver. The Sword creates the demarcation between sea and sky, and it is that thin silver strand of white, sandy beach which separates those two deep blue-grey realms when the voyager returns home from voyaging.

After this come the nine beads of the Eternal Sea. The surrounding ocean is the source of mysterious things. It is the realm which encompasses and conceals foreign lands, protects the land from invasions, and holds the roots of Sacred Land in its womb. The sea is constantly changing, yet changeless. It may create or destroy land, both by virtue of its motion. It is a rich source of food and plenty, and yet may kill those who venture upon it.

Our final turn through the manifest realms leads us to the Treasure of Murias, Coire Ansic (*kweer*-ah *an*-sick, "un-dry cauldron") the Cauldron of Daghda and its accompanying winds. Its guardian is Semias. This Treasure contains all the endless sea, and stands between the waters of birth and the consumption of death and resurrection or rebirth. The word "un-dry" is not a title so much as the description of a state of constant fullness and plenty.

With this Treasure, we come full circle, from the act of Danu, giving birth to all the sacred realms, to the act of Bile, guiding and guarding the spirit on its way to the realm of rest and the dead.

We then return to the Double Spiral Gate and descend the dangling strand of the Inner Flame to the Gate of Divine Mysteries which began our voyage of cosmology and discovery. We return to the source from which all wisdom flows, and are, perhaps, a little wiser for the journey.

9

Building
the
Circle

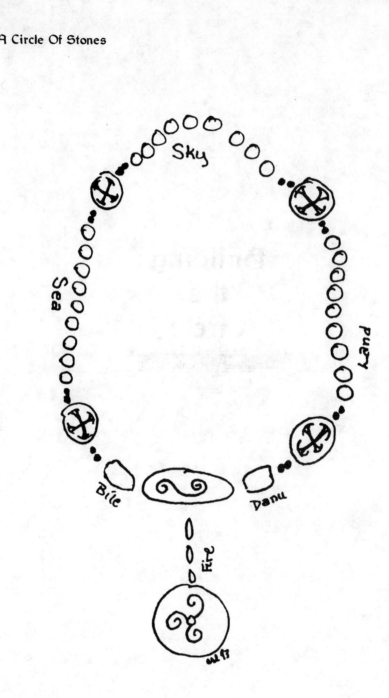

To make your own Circle of Stones, you will need beads, a needle, some glue, and strong beading cord. Stone, bone, wood, or glass beads are preferable. You may want to get a book on basic beading techniques as well. Glass is a good material because of the wide variety of colors, shapes and textures available. Stone is more expensive and tends to be much heavier. Wood is good because it is inexpensive, very light, and comes in a variety of shapes and colors. Any metal beads or medallions should be made of silver, brass or bronze. According to Celtic mythology, iron, and presumably its alloys, interferes with magic. Along with the beads which symbolize specific things, you should have a good supply of smaller beads to use as spacers to make the circle easier to handle.

The cord will need to be strong enough to withstand a lot of handling. Waxed cord will be stronger than unwaxed. Refer to the accompanying illustration for details on positioning the beads.

Your Circle of Stones may be as plain or ornate as you desire. Spend time looking for beads that are pleasing to the eye and interesting to the touch. The cost of basic materials may be as low as $20, but if you want special beads of imported glass or semi-precious stone, be prepared to spend upwards of $40. A good size for the beads of the three realms is 10mm to 14mm, although larger is certainly possible. At this size, using larger beads to represent the four treasures, you might be able to wear your circle as a necklace. Smaller beads would make a circle of a good size to fit in your pocket or purse.

Choose seed beads of a color that compliments the rest of your beads for spacing. You will be putting these between each bead to give you more space to handle the circle as you meditate. Three or five beads can be used between the different types of beads, for instance between the wind beads and the realm beads. This will give your fingers a tactile clue that you have reached the end of a series.

It is easiest to make the section with the Gate of Divine Mysteries and the Inner Flame separately, and then attach them to the body of the circle. Make knots between each group of beads so that if your strand should break at some point, you will lose fewer of them, and your entire circle won't fall apart.

The Gate of Divine Mysteries should be a large stone, medallion or bead, preferably triangular or circular. You can paint

Triskeles
left spinning
Tuathail
right spinning
Deosil

or engrave it with a triskele on one side, and the "Fionn's Window" glyph on the other, should you so desire. It can be any color you like.

Above these are the three beads of the Inner Flame. They should be red, or a deep red-orange. Carnelian, red agates, or garnet are all appropriate.

The Double Spiral Gate may be a convenient holey-stone, or a large oblong bead or medallion which might be painted or

Double Spirals

engraved with a double spiral. There are a number of variants on the double spiral which are shown in the accompanying illustrations.

To the right of the Double Spiral Gate is a large dark colored bead which represents Danu. This may be amber, jet, bone, or wood. These are appropriate because they are all things which were once alive in one form or another.

Next are two beads which are slightly larger than your spacers, but not as large as the beads representing the three realms. They should be a distinctively different color or shape than the spacing beads. Clear or cloudy crystal would be good. These are two of the four winds which surround the bead representing the Treasure.

Each of the four Treasures should look approximately alike, but need not be identical. You may wish to use long oblong bone or wood beads, or metal medallions engraved or painted with an equal-armed Celtic cross, or with four-fold knotwork or Pictish key patterns. Circles or squares are appropriate shapes for the Treasure beads. Four-fold knotwork also comes in a variety of forms, some of which are illustrated to aid the imagination.

After each Treasure are two more wind beads.

Following the wind beads are nine beads representing Sacred Land. These may be deep green, brown, black, or some other

Fourfold Patterns

earthy color. Jet, tigereye, moss agate, black onyx, picture jasper, or other similar stones are all good.

The beads for Endless Sky should be blue. This may be a deep blue, like sodalite, or speckled lapis lazuli, or it might be a lighter blue like holley blue agate or a blue quartz variety. White or grey can also be appropriate, as the colors of mist and cloud.

Eternal Sea should be light green or blue-green. Malachite, jade, aquamarine, periodot and green turquoise are all appropriate colors. The ocean itself is a deep green color on stormy days.

At the end, the bead for Bile should approximately match the Danu bead in size and shape, but should be a lighter color. Wood, amber, horn, antler or bone would all work nicely. Once again, these are materials that were once living. This bead should be attached to the Double Spiral Gate, completing your circle.

Using
the
Circle

Now that you have built your Circle of Stones, what should you do with it?

Each segment symbolizes a different part of Celtic cosmology. In the next chapter are poems to recite and meditations to do with your circle that correspond to each section of beads.

The basic technique is quite simple. In the morning when you awaken, or at night before you go to bed, hold the circle in your hands. Take a few moments to calm your mind and think about what you are going to do. Beginning with the Gate of Divine Mysteries, hold each bead and recite the poetry that goes along with it.

For sections with many beads, repeat the poetry as you hold each bead, moving along the strand in a counter-clockwise direction. This direction seems to have been one of bringing power into manifestation among the early Irish Celts.

The poetry is provided in both English and Gaelic.[3] I recommend trying the Gaelic, as the rhythm and internal rhyme is much more beautiful and hypnotic. A rough pronunciation guide is provided at the end of the book.

Take your time as you go through the series of poems. There is no need to hurry. In fact, it is better if you move through the poetry slowly, considering the meaning of the words and thinking about the symbols.

You will find that the poetry is more effective when recited aloud. Its rhythm becomes much more clear, and the way that the words roll off the tongue can be quite sensual and delightful.

Given time, you will find that the poems begin to come naturally. If you repeat your meditations every day, you will eventually memorize the poems without even trying, and then you will be able to meditate on the meaning without having to read the book as you go. This will release you to do more complex work with the circle and its poetry. Some of these more advanced techniques, like journeying into Otherworld realms, are described in later chapters.

The
Daily
Round

The Gate of Divine Mysteries

Here is the secret gate, the opening of the way. It is the beginning of the journey, of immram to the sacred land. A journey must begin with a desire to attain the goal, and our goal is the divine wisdom of mythic Ireland. Our source is the hidden source of the Well of Wisdom, navel of Danu, tended by the Goddess Boann. At our beginning is a Name -- the tri-fold Name of the Sovereignty of Ireland: Fodla, Banbha, Eriu. These are the cunning wives of Bres, of Buaigne. With these Names we can begin our search, rising through the triple eddies of the waters in Tobhair Segais.

Ailiu iath nErend.	I invoke the land of Ireland.
Ermach muir mothuch,	Much-coursed be the fertile sea,
Mothach silagh sreathach,	Fertile be the fruit-strewn mountain,
Srethach coill ciothoch,	Fruit-strewn be the showery wood,
Ciothach ab essach,	Showery be the river of waterfalls,
Eassach loch lionnmar,	Of waterfalls be the lake of deep pools,
Liondmar tor tiopra,	Deep-pooled be the hill-top well,
Tiopra tuath aenagh,	A well of tribes be the assembly,
Aenach righ Temra,	An assembly of kings be Tara,
Teamair tor tuatha,	Tara be a hill of the tribes,
Tuatha mac Miled,	The tribes of the sons of Mil,
Miledh long, libern,	Of Mil of the ships, the barks,
Libern ard, Ére,	Let the lofty bark be Ireland,
Ére ard, diclass,	Lofty Ireland, darkly sung,
Dichteal rogaeth:	An incantation of great cunning:
Ro gaes ban Breisi,	The great cunning of the wives of Bres,
Breisi, ban Buaigni;	The wives of Bres, of Buaigne;
Be abdal Ére,	The great lady Ireland,
Eremhón ortus,	Eremon hath conquered her,
Ir, Ebir ailsius.	Ir, Eber have invoked for her.
Ailiu iath nErenn.[4]	I invoke the land of Ireland.

Moving Meditations on the Gate of Divine Mysteries

Find the roots of something
Trace your family genealogy
Look for the etymology of a word or a name
Study techniques of invocation
Learn about Celtic well-dressing customs
Read a creation myth
Begin a quest for something

Affirmation for the Gate of Divine Mysteries

Today I invoke my own inner sacred place:
a land fertile with creativity, a well deep with wisdom, and a sky
showery with many blessings.

The Inner Flame

Sparking, rising through the Well of Wisdom and linking the three realms is the bright pillar of the Inner Flame. It is the indwelling spirit of our Tree of Life, our Cosmic Pillar[5] holding up the sky. It is the nail around which the heavens revolve. The three beads of flame are our watchfires, and the three internal cauldrons of meditation[6] -- the Cauldron of Warmth, the Cauldron of Motion, and the Cauldron of Wisdom. Breathing through them, we reach for the transforming power of the flames.

Go gcosnai tinte fhaire Temair muid ag na-hoibre

Let the watch-flames of Tara guard us in our work

Go ndo tinnáil rabhaidh Temair muid a ghiollacht tri na scáileanna

Let the signal-fires of Tara burn to guide us through the shadows

Go lasa laistigh bruane coronach Temair agus ceangail muid le na dheithe[7]

Let the crowning flames of Tara spark within and link us to the Gods.

Moving Meditations on the Inner Flame

Study the role of flame in Celtic mythology
Work on candle meditations
Dance around a bonfire
Observe your breathing
Study Yoga or a martial art, paying special attention to
"chi" or "kundalini"
Write a poem
Compose a song
Choreograph a dance
Light and tend a sacred fire on your altar

Affirmation for the Inner Flame

Today I create the sacred flame of inspiration
within myself, linking the inner spark of my soul
with that greater bonfire that manifests deity.

The Double Spiral Gate

Here is the spiral gate of Life and Death. It is the two High Days of the year, Samhain at the beginning of night, and Beltain, the day's bright dawn. The Double Spiral Gate represents the ebb and flow of time, and the passage of life and death. By flow and beginning we approach the Goddess Danu to begin the journey through the manifest realms.

Tonn tuili	The flood-wave
ocus ind i aithbi áin:	and that of swift ebb:
a ndo-beir tonn tuili dait	what the flood-wave brings you
beirid tonn aithbi as do láim	the ebb-wave carries out of your hand
Tonn tuili	The flood-wave
ocus ind aile aithbe:	and that second wave which is ebb:
dom-áncatarsa uili	all have come to me
conda éolach a n-aithgni[8]	so that I know and control them

Moving Meditations on the Double Spiral Gate

Meditate on the meanings of evening as the start of day,
and Samhain as the year's beginning
Sit and watch a sunset
Examine the "gateway" points in your life and catalogue
your significant personal and spiritual beginnings
Read about the initiatory process
Participate in the birth of someone or something
Learn the art of drumming, and meditate on the use rhythm
as a gateway

Affirmation for the Double Spiral Gate

Today I acknowledge the sacred flow of time;
beginning and ending;
flow and ebb;
the gateway which brings all things to birth.

Danu

Danu, source of the Land, stands at the beginning of the manifest. Through Her we experience our birth, and She is mother to the Gods as well as to we who seek Her. Her mysteries are those of beginnings. She is unmanifest, yet the source of all that is. She is herself the solidity of the Otherworld realms.

Co i bhain-tighearna bhinn,
am bun an tuim,
am beul an tuim?

Who is she the melodious Lady,
at the base of the knoll,
at the mouth of the wave?

Ban-tigearna bhinn
Bhaindidh mhin.[9]

Melodious Lady,
As a Goddess in loveliness.

Moving Meditations on Danu

Study the Celtic Earth-Goddesses and Mother-Goddesses
in all their manifestations
Do a daily devotion to Danu or your personal Goddess
Do a weekly devotion to a different Celtic Goddess
Find or create a Goddess image for your home or altar
Spend time outside listening to the voice of your Goddess
Give comfort to yourself and those around you
Allow someone to nurture you
Meditate on dusk as the beginning of the day

Affirmation for Danu

Today I will look for the Goddess in all that I do
and all that I see;
Her face in every face, Her presence in all places,
Her love surrounding me,
embracing and upholding me.

The West Wind

The west wind is the hard wind from over the ocean. It blows bringing plenty, carrying the fishing fleets back from the shoals. This wind carries those who come seeking the Land, to conquer or to settle, from beyond the Ninth Wave.

Gaoth an iar iasg is aran;
Gaoth a tuath fuachd is feannadh;

Gaoth an ear sneachd air beannaibh;

Gaoth a deas meas air crannaibh.[10]

Wind from the west, fish and bread;
Wind from the north,
     cold and flaying;

Wind from the east,
     snow on the hills;

Wind from the south, fruit on trees.

Moving Meditations on the West Wind

Go to an aquarium and watch the fish for an afternoon
Look for the conquests in your life, appreciating those
you have made and planning for those you await
Walk in the wind blowing from the west
Meditate on something recently arrived in your life
Work on conquering one of your fears
Go fishing

Affirmation for the West Wind

Today I conquer that which hinders
my progress through life

Lia Fail

Lia Fail is the symbol of the Land and of its fulfillment. At the Stone of Fal the Kings of Ireland were crowned, and its scream confirmed the identity of the one who was fated to join in the sacred marriage of Sovereignty of the Land and the Ardh Righ, the high king.

An cloch forsttád mo di sáil,
uaithe raiter Inis Fáil:
etir da triagh tuile tinn
Magh fáil uile for Eirinn.[11]

The stone on which my heels stand,
From it is named Inis Fál;
Between two strands of a mighty flood
All Ireland is called the Plain of Fál.

Moving Meditations for Lia Fail

Learn about the symbolism and magical use of gems,
crystals, and stones
Study the alignment of standing stones
and stone monuments
Investigate the geology of your area
Learn to identify the many different kinds of stones
Find and consecrate your own "Lia Fail"
Read about Sacred Marriages and sacred Kingship

Affirmation for the Lia Fail

Today I know and accept that I rule my life
and choose my fate;
no other may hold my sovereign sacred place,
no other may reign over my spirit or the land which is my life.

Sacred Land

This is the Land of the physical realm. It is more than merely Ireland as one parcel of land, it is the entire manifest physical universe. All land is sacred land, and our connection to the Land is our stability. Sacred Land underlies all of our magical reality, surrounded and bounded by the Eternal Sea.

Coic urranna hErenn
etir muir agus tír
Addeoch-sa na coem canle
cacha cóicid díb[12]

The five parts of Ireland
between sea and land
I entreat the fair candles
of every province among them

Moving Meditations on Sacred Land

Walk barefoot in the grass
Plant and tend a garden or a windowbox
Read about the history of your local area and its
native people
Adopt a park and help keep it clean
Learn the medicinal or magical uses of an herb
Work for the preservation of a sacred site
Do a daily grounding exercise
Study the Gaia Theory
Take a course on local ecology

Affirmation for the Sacred Land

Today I affirm that I and the Land are One.

The South Wind

The south wind is the soft, warm wind of summer. It brings warmth and growth, softening the land and giving ease to the heart. On the south wind is the scent of blooming flowers and the ripening odor of fruit on the trees.

Gaoth an iar iasg is aran;
Gaoth a tuath fuachd is feannadh;

Gaoth an ear sneachd air beannaibh;

Gaoth a deas meas air crannaibh.[13]

Wind from the west, fish and bread;
Wind from the north,
        cold and flaying;
Wind from the east,
        snow on the hills;
Wind from the south, fruit on trees.

Moving Meditations on the South Wind

Savor summer berries
Put sweet scented flowers on your altar
Burn a summery incense
Meditate in a southerly wind
Eat spicy foods
Read about Celtic Gods and Goddesses
with solar attributes
Take a hot, scented bubble bath

Affirmation for the South Wind

Today I appreciate the fruitfulness of my life,
Giving myself the warmth of love

The Spear of Lugh

Lugh's spear is unassailable assurance of victory, for none can stand against its might. With this Treasure wielded on our behalf, we progress on our journey unhindered by dangers from the spiritual realm.

Agus Lugh caomh-gheal,
    cro-gheal, cra-gheal,
Ga do dhiona, ga do chaomhna,
    ga do charamh
Le treuin a laimhe, le nimh a ghaise,

Fo sgaile drilleanach a sgeith.[14]

And may Lugh kind-white,
    strong-white, red-white
Preserve thee, protect thee,
    provide for thee,
With the might of his hand, with the
    point of his spear,
Under the shade of his shimmering
    shield.

Moving Meditation for the Spear of Lugh

Learn a new art or skill
Study defensive magical techniques
Do a devotional to Lugh
Read the tale of the Second Battle of Magh Tuiredh
Research the occurrences of the names Lugh, Lug, Llew
and other variants in Celtic mythologies
Protect someone if they are in danger

Affirmation for the Spear of Lugh

Today I see and appreciate my many talents.

Endless Sky

The boundless sky overarches all our lives, defining the dome of the heavens. It holds the patterns of the stars that reveal mysteries dancing through the night, and the sun and moon in their eternal circling. The Tuatha de Danann sailed through this realm in their boats on the winds, and the sky is the center from which all the winds have their origin.

Is tu grian nan néamha,	Thou art the sun of the heavens,
Is tu gile nan speura,	Thou art the moon of the skies,
Is tu reul agus ceuma	Thou art the star and the path
Nam faontrach.[15]	Of the wanderers.

Moving Meditations for
the Endless Sky

Learn the names of the stars and constellations
Find out how to read the clouds to predict the weather
Study astrology
Learn about local species of birds
Lie on your back and watch the clouds or the stars
Discover when the next meteor shower is due and watch
for the falling stars
Do rituals to mark the solar and lunar cycles
Construct a sundial
Put out a bird feeder or bath

Affirmations for the Endless Sky

Today I know that I am made of the stuff of stars

41

The East Wind

The east wind is the sharp, cold wind that cuts and brings the snows. It brings dawn and the morning light. This wind is the origin of inspiration and enlightenment in the material realm.

Gaoth an iar iasg is aran;
Gaoth a tuath fuachd is feannadh;

Gaoth an ear sneachd air beannaibh;

Gaoth a deas meas air crannaibh.[16]

Wind from the west, fish and bread;
Wind from the north,
    cold and flaying;
Wind from the east,
    snow on the hills;
Wind from the south, fruit on trees.

Moving Meditations on the East Wind

Walk in an east wind
Look at snowflakes and meditate on their form
Watch a sunrise from a hilltop
Discover a source of inspiration in your life
Meditate on the quality of "sharpness" and its meanings
and metaphors
Examine the places in your life where you act in a sharp
or cold manner and learn to appreciate their strengths
and weaknesses

Affirmation for the East Wind

Today I embrace the cold and the sharp;
I move with their bracing vigor.

The Sword of Nuadha

This is the Sword which cuts the boundary between Sea and Sky, the razor's edge of silver beach. The sword of light shines with brightness unbearable, protecting and defining the boundaries which we can only touch in the briefest of those moments which we spend in the neither-nor spaces between.

Claíomh gheur, ghlan,	A sword keen, true
Gun smal, gun smur,	Without stain, without dust,
Gun sal, gun sur,	Without smear, without flaw,
Gun mhur, gun mheirg.[17]	Without grime, without rust.

Moving Meditation for the Sword of Nuadha

Take fencing lessons
Study the concept of liminality and
the importance of boundaries
Do devotionals to Nuadha
Examine your spiritual or emotional wounds
and seek wholeness
Read myths of the wounded king

Affirmation for the Sword of Nuadha

Today I acknowledge the wounds I bear,
Yet I seek to heal those wounds

Eternal Sea

The Sea is the boundary which defines the Land, encircling the material realm and creating the barrier between our realm and the realm of the Gods. Here is the place between, the Ninth Wave beyond which we cannot go without the aid of strong Gods. It contains the Nine Wells of Manannan mac Lir and at its bottom lies the well of wisdom, with the strength and the restless power of endless motion.

Muir mor, muir glas
Neart mara, neart cuain,

Naoi tobraiche Mhic-a-Lir[18]

Great wave, green wave,
Strength of sea,
     strength of ocean
The nine wells of Mac Lir

Moving Meditations for the Eternal Sea

Learn to sail a boat
Meditate on the sea as the boundary of the world
Watch for the changing of the tides
and study how the moon affects them
Watch storms come in from the sea
Wade in the waves
Find driftwood and shells for your altar
Build sand sidhe mounds

Affirmation for the Eternal Sea

Today I explore, acknowledge and appreciate my limits

The North Wind

This is the wind from the North of the world. The north wind is the bringer of magic, the essence of newness. It is the lazy wind, which moves through, rather than going around whatever is in its way.

Gaoth an iar iasg is aran;
Gaoth a tuath fuachd is feannadh;

Gaoth an ear sneachd air beannaibh;

Gaoth a deas meas air crannaibh.[19]

Wind from the west, fish and bread;
Wind from the north,
cold and flaying;
Wind from the east,
snow on the hills;
Wind from the south, fruit on trees.

Moving Meditations on the North Wind

Meditate on newness
Look at the world with the eyes of a child
Seek out that which is hidden
Walk in the wind as it blows from the north
Find the meaning and the source of power in your life
Perform a magical act
Confront the different forms of laziness in your life
Cut through confusion to the heart of something

Affirmation for the North Wind

Today I will allow the magic in life
to manifest through me.

Coire Ansic

Here is the Cauldron of Daghda which can never be emptied, from which none goes away unsatisfied. Coire Ansic contains the ocean, and the streams running into and out of it from their source at the Well of Wisdom are the senses with which we perceive the world and the life around us. This Otherworld gift contains all knowledge and all healing, inexhaustible gifts for the seeker.

Ara-caun Coire Sofhis
sernar dliged cach dáno
dia moiget moín
móras cach ceird coitchiunn
con-utaing duine dán[20]

I acclaim the Cauldron of Knowledge
where the law of every art is set out
which makes prosperity
which magnifies every artist
which exalts a person by means of art

Moving Meditations on Coire Ansic

Practice sacred hospitality
Concentrate on one of your senses and listen deeply
to what it is telling you
Donate to a food bank
Do a devotional to Daghda
Experience something to the fullest
Study a healing art
Give a friend a gift for no particular reason
Appreciate the generosity of others

Affirmation for Coire Ansic

Today I see the generous nature of the universe
and honor my obligation of hospitality

Bile

Tall and strong as the pale-white birch is Bile, roots in the Land but reaching to the Sky. Bile stands at the gates of Life and Death, welcoming us home as we leave our bodies in the material realm. He is our guardian and our guide through the House of Donn to the Otherworld realm beyond. We meet him at the place where Land, Sea and Sky meet as one, on the silver sand under the moon of midnight, dwelling within the mists.

In fial fortail, arcech fintóir,
In slíab dergóir.
In dorr bítnes dronga,
Don chlár chathbath.[21]

The munificent lord of every succor,
The mountain of red gold.
The tree which wards the multitudes
Off the death-battle plain.

Moving Meditations on Bile

Plant a tree that is appropriate to your local ecology
Study Celtic Otherworld beliefs
Make a will
Find your own sacred grove
Read and meditate on the processes of
dying, death and grief
Do daily devotionals to Bile or your personal God
Do a devotional to a different Celtic God each week
Learn about Celtic tree lore
Create an altar for your ancestors

Affirmation for Bile

Today I see the God in nature;
Sacred trees, holy springs,
Beauty in the cycle of the seasons

The Double Spiral Gate

Here we return to the spiral gate of Life and Death. We pass through it again after we have experienced the ebb and flow of time, and the passage of life and death. By ebb and ending we depart from the of the manifest realms and return, with the aid of Manannan the gatekeeper, through the swirling, rising mists to the source of all things.

Tonn tuili	The flood-wave
ocus ind i aithbi áin:	and that of swift ebb:
a ndo-beir tonn tuili dait	what the flood-wave brings you
beirid tonn aithbi as do láim	the ebb-wave carries out of your hand
Tonn tuili	The flood-wave
ocus ind aile aithbe:	and that second wave which is ebb:
dom-áncatarsa uili	all have come to me
conda éolach a n-aithgni[22]	so that I know and control them

Moving Meditations on the Double Spiral Gate

Assess your life, both positive and negative experiences,
and make peace with who you are today
Meditate on the mists between the worlds
Do a devotional to Manannan the gatekeeper
Sit and watch the ebbing tide
Study the significance of gates
and doorways in mythology
Read the Celtic *immrama* tales

Affirmation for the Double Spiral Gate

Today I acknowledge the sacred flow of time;
ending and beginning;
ebb and flow;
the gateway which takes all things past death

The Inner Flame

As we return through the realm of death to the source and to the Otherworld, we pass once again the watchfires which we invoked at the beginning of our journey. These flames light our way, defining the boundaries of our exploration, showing us our links to land and deities, and enlightening us through meditation and the spark of poetic inspiration.

Chosain tinte fhaire Temair muid ag na-hoibre	The watch-flames of Tara have guarded our work
Dhoigh tinnáil rabhaidh Temair muid aghoiollacht tri na scáileanna	The signal fires of Tara have guided us through the shadows
Lasannaigh laistigh bruane coronach Temair agus ceangail muid le na dheithe.[23]	The crowing flames of Tara leap within and have linked us to the Gods.

Moving Meditations on the Inner Flame

Read and ponder on the seasonal fires of Beltain,
Samhain and Lughnassadh
Meditate on the connections between humans,
the land and the deities
Study the three harp strains of joy, sorrow and sleep,
and how they may relate to the internal cauldrons
Examine Celtic poetic metres, how they are constructed,
and how they are used

Affirmation for the Inner Flame

Today I stand between the sacred flames, purified,
prepared to meet the deities in their own lands

The Gate of Divine Mysteries

At the end of our search for sacred land and identity, we find ourselves looking into the mirror. Our search brings us full circle back to ourselves, more developed, more capable, in control of our lives and our surroundings. Our experiences in the sacred realms have taught us, and by learning we have achieved growth. The ultimate riddle boils down to "who am I?" and this riddle has only one answer. With this question, we seek, and we learn, our true Name.

Am goeth i muir
am tonn trethain
am fuaim mara
am dam setir
am seg for aill
am der greine
am cain luba
am torc an gail
am eo i lindibh
am loch i maigh
am brigh dana
am gai la fodb feras feachta
am dae delbus do chind cotnu
Coiche notglen clochar slebe?

Cia du i luidh fúinedh greiniu?
Cia seacht siecht gan eccla?

Cia non dogar eassa uissci?
Cia ber a buar o tigh Teathra?

Cia buar Tethrach tibide?
Cia doen, cia dia,
dealbus faebra andiond?
Indiond ailes cainte:
Dichain tothlach, diales fedha,

fodhail coblach, cachain aille,
ailiside sieas coimes cainte,
cainte gaith.[24]

I am a wind on the sea
I am a wave of the ocean
I am the roar of the sea
I am a powerful stag
I am a hawk on a cliff
I am a dewdrop in the sunshine
I am the most delicate of herbs
I am a boar for valor
I am a salmon in a pool
I am a lake in a plain
I am the strength of art
I am a spear with spoil waging battle
I am a God who shapes fire for a head
Who clears the stony places in the
    mountains?
In what place lies the setting of the sun?
Who has sought peace without fear
    seven times?
Who names the waterfalls?
Who brings the cattle from the house
    of Tethra?
On whom do the cattle of Tethra smile?
What person, what God
Forms weapons in a fort?
In a fort that nourishes satirists,
Chants a petition, divides the
    ogham letters,
Separates a fleet, has sung praises,
Weighs chants and invocations
Sings enchantments for spears.

Moving Meditations on the Gate of Divine Mysteries

Study riddles and their answers
Find your magical name
Learn about the significance of heads in Celtic religion
Meditate on the Fionn's Window glyph
Read stories of shapeshifting deities and magicians
Study the different theories of reincarnation
and transmigration
"Who am I?" - keep a journal of self-exploration

Affirmation for the Gate of Divine Mysteries

Today I name myself in the realm of the Gods

Rites
of
Devotion

Creating Rituals

Devotionals are ritual acts and meditations that are designed to focus your attention on a particular deity or group of deities. These rituals express connections between you and your Gods and Goddesses. They can also be done for Ancestors, as they often are in Shinto and other "ancestor worshipping" religions. Rituals of devotion to land spirits are common in folk religions like the Celtic "fairy faith."

A devotional is not a ritual that asks for something. A ritual for prosperity is not a devotional rite, nor is a love spell or a protection spell. Instead, the rite places you firmly within a relationship between yourself and your deities. Ancestor devotions are done to reaffirm your link with friends, family and significant people who have gone to the House of Donn, as well as the unknown and unnamed ancients who walked Pagan paths before you, and to remind them that you are still thinking of them. Land spirit devotionals are often done to gain a better relationship with them, and to prevent any mischief they might be prone to cause.

Devotions to deities are performed to gain a better understanding of the deity, and the Gods and Goddesses will often share information with their devotees. Through the process of your rituals you will discover things that the deities are associated with, what they like, and also the things that displease them and which you should avoid. Researching and preparing a devotional ritual shows the deities that you are actively interested in interacting with them, and it may call their attention to you in a positive manner.

Reading and meditation are important before you begin to design your altar and your devotional rituals. Both are necessary and will give you the basics of symbolism for setting your altar, and the names and some of the titles by which your chosen deities should be addressed. Your work will reveal tales and material which can become the basis for the words of your devotional rites, as well as the conditions and situations in which each deity is most often encountered. A devotional can of course be done with no props other than your intent, particularly when very little is known about a deity. Using linking symbols, if they are available, is always helpful.

Preparation is no guarantee of instant success, but neither is sincerity alone. Time and effort are both important ingredients for your devotional work. The nature of spiritual work and development is slow and painstaking. Success will undoubtedly come, but you must reach for it and put your best effort into your workings. Always remember that what you get out of your devotional rituals will be dependent upon what you put into them. Your effort may be great, but your rewards will be greater.

Here is a sample devotional ritual for Danu. It is very simple in structure, but the amount of symbol and emotional involvement is rich and deep.

Devotional Rite for the Goddess Danu

Items needed:
dark green candle
incense burner
incense of cedar and fir
votive candles & holders
offerings of food and drink
image or symbol of Danu
ancestor and land spirit images or objects
objects to represent the three realms of land, sea and sky

Assemble the items for your rite in a convenient place. This may be at one of your altars where you live, or it might be somewhere outdoors. Either place is fine, but be sure you will be comfortable and that you will be in a place where you will feel safe and not be disturbed by anyone.

Address Manannan the Gatekeeper and ask his aid in crossing into the Otherworld. After you have done this, assemble your altar. It should be at a convenient height for standing, or if you prefer it lower, make it convenient for sitting either in a chair or on a cushion. Celtic deities prefer that people come before them with pride and in honor, so we do not usually kneel to them.

Place the image of Danu in the north, arranging the Three Realms with the sky in the north, sea in the southwest and land in the southeast. Put the incense burner and the dark green candle in front of Danu. Put small bowls for food and drink before her as well.

Ancestor images should, if possible, go in the southwest, near your sea objects. Place votive candles before them, along with little bowls for food and drink.

Land spirit images and items should go near your land objects, but can be placed anywhere you like so long as they aren't in the way. They also should have little bowls available for food and drink offerings. If you like, you can have votive candles for them, but it isn't necessary.

Prepare yourself for your contact with the Goddess by doing focussed breathing meditations, or any other technique you like.

Begin by addressing the ancestors. Ask their attendance and thank them for coming. Put food and drink into the bowls in front of them and light the votive candles for them, meditating for a while on their presence. Ask their help in coming before the Goddess Danu, as they are closer to her than we are by already being in the Otherworld realms.

Address the land spirits next, offering them food and drink as well. Thank them for their support and their kindness to you, allowing you to prosper in their domains. Meditate here as well. You may wish to hold and look at your land spirit objects at this time -- leaves, stones, nuts or dried berries, things that you have picked up during your rituals to honor them -- turn them over in your hands to feel their texture, smell leaves and remember where you gathered them, let seeds or sand run between your fingers. Ask the land spirits to make your way clear as you call upon Danu.

Light the incense. Draw the double spiral gate in front of the image with your finger or with the incense. Call out to Danu, "A Dhanu, Ban-tiarna! A Dhanu, mo Bandia!" [ah Yah-noo, bahn-tyer-na, ah Yah-noo, muh bahn-jyah, "Danu, Lady! Danu, my Goddess!"] Invoke her with your own words, with drumming, chanting poetry from the circle meditations, or singing until you begin to feel her presence. Don't rush this process. Enjoy the invocation as much as you enjoy the Goddess herself. Light the candle and give her food and drink offerings.

When she has come to you and you have made your offerings, take time to sing, dance, play music, write or recite praise poetry to her, or do other things that seem appropriate. Make noise, be joyful. Tell her you love her.

If you prefer quiet, you can meditate in her presence focussing on your image or symbol. Seek her moods, listen to her voice, walk with her through the forest, drink from her waters. Even if you perform an active and noisy devotional rite, spend some time in quiet contemplation before you close the ritual.

Spend as much time in the presence of Danu as you wish, or as she decides. Thank her for coming to you and for sharing her presence and her wisdom with you. Tell her that she may stay and inhabit your altar or return to her own realm as she pleases. Watch and feel to determine if she stays or leaves. If Danu has gone, you can put her candle out. If she has not, let it burn for several more hours and leave her food and drink offerings on the altar after you have ended the ritual. Seven day candles are generally safe in their glass containers and should not cause problems when left alone, so long as cats or other small creatures are not allowed to mess with them.

Thank the ancestors and land spirits. Tell them you will invite them to spend time with you again soon, and put out the votive candles.

Take the food and drink offerings outside when you are finished and pour them out or bury them somewhere where they won't be disturbed.

As you can see, this ritual is very easily modified to suit any deity, and similar rituals can be done for ancestors and land spirits as well. Being simple, it is suited to endless variations according to mood and purpose. It is suggested that you begin with rituals only for your personal deities until you have some familiarity with the ways that deity can manifest. Trying to work with too many deities all at once is distracting and will detract from your experiences. Being able to focus on a few deities will give you a greater depth of understanding and allow you to expand your knowledge and range of experience with time.

Remember that true spirituality doesn't mean you've joined the Deity of the Month Club. What it does mean is that you have devoted yourself to living with the Gods as a part of your life, and that you are seeking to understand and experience them in ways that you can integrate into your daily existence. Ritual is a valuable and powerful tool to achieve this goal. Consistency pays off in the gold and fire of wisdom.

On the Making of Altars

The first step toward creating and doing a devotional rite for Ancestors, land spirits or a deity is the construction of your altar. An altar is not so much a thing, as it is a way of arranging and relating the images and symbols from your meditations and the deities as they manifest and make sense to you. Spatial relationships become important as they express how the various energies and symbols interact.

Each altar you construct will be unique. They will have different purposes and will reveal and relate different complexes of symbols. An altar for your Ancestors will have a very different look and feel than an altar for your personal deity. Your altar will change as time passes, in response to your changing needs and understandings. Other factors will influence your altar construction as well, reflecting your changing seasonal, situational, and magical concerns. Despite the many differing altar components and their changes, all altars will follow a few basic rules of construction.

When designing your altar, start with a theme and structure everything else around it. This theme may be a particular deity, or it might be a season or a particular goal that you have. For devotional rituals, the theme will usually be a deity, the Ancestors, or your local land spirits. The altar should include symbolism that represents the object of your devotional work through its construction, its positioning, and the objects that you arrange upon it. The items that make up your altar space should be related to one another symbolically, reflecting the focus of your devotional work, and the means through which you will accomplish the devotion. An altar doesn't have to be a flat surface. It can be three dimensional or multi-leveled. It can be built on a vertical rather than a horizontal plane.

When constructing an altar for a ritual of devotion to Manannan, you might include triskeles, ocean symbols, a coracle, a basket of apples, cranes, or yellow irises. This can take many different forms. The "altar" might be an alder staff which has been washed in sea water, with triskeles and a coracle engraved upon it which is then set upright into the ground as a focal point for your meditations. It could be a series of stones in your back yard arranged in a triskele formation, with a bowl of ocean water at its center, and ringed by apples. You might have a small table or corner shelf in your room that has a drawing of Manannan upon it, with a sprig of apple blossoms, shells, a small crane statue, a model boat and a container of sea salt. All of these objects are related thematically to the God Manannan, yet each is a different manifestation of the symbols which reflect an Otherworld reality. Each can be used as a focus for ritual in a unique and useful way. Creativity is important for expressing your individual understanding and responses to the symbols use.

You do not have to have only one altar. If you have the inclination, your entire living space and the landscape around you can be filled with sacred places, or become one large sacred space, devoted to recognizing a pattern that expresses your world view. A few inches of shelf space may become a shrine to a favorite ancestor, or a wall sconce devoted to a particular deity and set with fresh flowers and a bowl of scented water. A few stones in the yard might serve as an altar for land spirits. The nature of altars is such that no one ever need know that you have constructed one. Others may perceive your altars merely as attractive decoration, or unusual artistic touches in your house or personal space.

Altars reflect an understanding of sacred space. The things on your altar represent your inner world and how it relates to both mundane and Otherworld reality as you perceive it. This expression of sacred space brings your inner world into physical manifestation. By placing objects that reflect your inner reality in a physically defined material space, you can work with and manipulate the symbols of your inner world and create changes within yourself, your relationships with deity, or in the Otherworld. The construction of your altar will reflect not only your understanding of your inner world and the Otherworld, but your interactions with and understanding of society at large. An altar can be a patch of ground, a stone, a table, a fireplace mantel, a set of shelves, a stang driven into the earth, or any number of other things. It might be round, square, triangular, or none of these.

Your altar doesn't have to be neat or tidy. It does have to work for you. It can be aesthetically pleasing and even artistic without being anal retentive or gridded into evenly spaced boxes. Break the tyranny of the rectangular altar space. Feel free to have as much or as little on your altar as you like. Arrangements can be orderly or chaotic, so long as you understand how and why you are putting things where they are. If you are more comfortable with a random scattering of twigs and a small statue than with an altar that came from a diagram in a book, then by all means use the looser altar setting. Working actively with your altars will result in a constantly shifting series of neatness and chaos reflecting your inner states and moods. Different levels of "neatness" work for different things, and you should be flexible enough in your altar arrangements to reflect these varying states.

The altar is a liminal place where our world and the Otherworld meet and interact. In this way, an altar can be thought of as a gateway from one realm to another, and the objects on the altar can be considered "between" places. Your altar is the *crann beithadh*, the "tree of life" upon which the Gods descend, and which holds up the sky. It is the sacred center which balances all divisions. The altar can be the literal center of the universe, the point where all things meet. Things and symbols upon the altar take on a different level of "reality" and small things may have great significance which belies their size. Your spiritual work and your magic will manifest in those places where the realms meet and overlap.

The altar expresses how things interact. The position of different symbols reflect their importance within the context of your inner world and your understanding of their action in the Otherworld. Cultural and religious understandings are expressed by the division and arrangement of symbols. Placing a thing in the center of an altar will give it a different emphasis than placing it at the back and to the right. Concepts such as sacred kingship, the relationship of humanity to the Gods, and the relation of humanity to the natural world can be expressed by placement of symbols within the sacred space of your altar. Arrangements can be dual/polar, triadic, quartered, or otherwise divided into a number of categories. Each arrangement will change the meaning of the things on the altar, according to where they are placed.

Dual or polar divisions can represent the polarity of masculine and feminine, of summer and winter, of day and night, of Samhain and Beltain. These can be expressed as left/right, up/down or back/front positioning, depending upon the size and configuration of your altar space. Triadic arrangements might express an understanding of triadic deity groupings (whether of the same or mixed gender), or your understandings of the three realms. A quartered arrangement might express movement from or to the directions, working with the winds, or representing the provinces of Ireland. The quartered arrangement is one that should be deeply meditated upon before using, because of its fluctuating nature within the different Celtic cosmologies, and its tendency to suddenly become a threefold or fivefold division without much warning.

Your altar shouldn't have to be dusted. Your workings should be frequent and varied enough that dusting becomes a superfluous act. The more work you do in your devotional rites, the more you will understand the structure of the Otherworld and your relationships to it. This in turn will lead to easier and more successful journeys through the Three Realms. A life of religious devotion need not take place in a hermitage or to the exclusion of your "mundane" daily activities. The symbols on your altar should integrate themselves into your life and allow you to act in harmony with the Gods and your personal goals. Working with these things on a frequent basis means that you are giving attention to the state of your inner life, acknowledging that it is at least as important as bringing home your next paycheck.

The altar is ultimately the place where you kindle the spark of imbas. Your personal energies are reflected and focused here, and the deities, Ancestors, and land spirits will be attracted to this focal point. Act accordingly, showing respect for yourself and for them. Don't embarrass the Gods, the spirits, or yourself around your altar.

To Speak With the Gods

How does one approach deity? Ideally, it is done with respect, openness, and a sense of the importance of your connection with the divine. Respect does not mean that you should grovel before the Gods. In fact, Celtic deities seem to singularly dislike that sort of behavior, and the moral codes of the Celts show that a certain amount of boasting and personal pride is not only to be expected, but actively encouraged.

Through your meditations with the Circle of Stones, you can focus your attention upon Danu, Bile or Manannan. With their assistance and cooperation, you will be introduced to the other Celtic deities.

Treat your meetings with and meditations upon the deities as you would an audience with someone you immensely admire and wish to learn from. Praise is appropriate, but only if you mean what you are saying. False praise is as insulting to the Gods as it is to your fellow mortals, and will likely result in your requests for information or assistance being ignored or actively resisted.

Know the names and titles of the deities you are inviting. It is only natural that you will receive a more positive response if you show that you know who you are talking to, rather than addressing a devotional to the spiritual equivalent of "hey, you!" Be aware that titles can often belong to several deities at once, and that the names and titles can shift with time and geography. If you intend to work with a particular deity, use as many names and titles as you can find. This will give you a better chance of actually invoking the deity that you want to interact with. Intention counts, even if you can't specifically identify an individual deity. Working with a set of deities a group rather than as discrete individuals, for instance deities associated with music, can be of some help, giving you an energy form to focus on without having to worry about exact names and personalities, which can be supplemented by your reading in the tales and poetry.

Precise naming is less important for the Ancestors, unless you wish to call upon some specific departed relative. You will probably want to specify that you are invoking your distant and perhaps unknown Pagan predecessors though, unless you are prepared to listen to a long lecture from your dead but devout Christian or Jewish relatives on how you are acting inappropriately. Remember that if you go back far enough in any family line, you will eventually run into Pagans. Even the relatives who lecture you about talking with spirits are likely to be happy that you are remembering and honoring them.

Land spirits often respond as a group rather than as individuals. It is still very important to be aware of the types of local land spirits that you will encounter, as they vary from region to region, both in temperament and in goals. If there is a substantial immigrant Celtic population, you may be fortunate enough to encounter Celtic land spirits who came with them, along with the native land spirits. These transplanted types will tend to be the spirits who lived on farmsteads or near households and were associated with mortals, and will almost never be the ones associated with specific kinds of places, such as wells, forests, or particular geographical features. You may run across spirits who are associated with particular families as well. Especially in following a Celtic path, it is important to acknowledge the spirits of the land in which you dwell. The land spirits can make your access to local energies easier, or they can hamper your work if they perceive you as hostile or an interloper.

In the Celtic world, hospitality is a sacred duty, and your first order of business. When inviting the Gods, Ancestors, or land spirits to your altar, it is appropriate and necessary to offer food and drink. This should be a portion apart from what you yourself are consuming, and should not be eaten afterwards. Celtic tradition has it that once the Gods or the spirits have had their fill, the *toradh*, the "substance" or spiritual essence of the food has been taken, and the remaining physical portion would be at best non-nutritious or at worst, actively harmful.

In Irish mythology, the preferred foods of Gods and spirits are such things as milk, ale, mead, hazel nuts, wine, apples, oats, rowan berries, butter, and pork. All these are well-attested in myths and folk tales. Any of them would be suitable offerings of hospitality to the deities who are receiving your devotional rites. For local land spirits, locally grown food is the best offering. If, for some reason, none of these things is available to you, the finest portion of whatever you have will certainly be acceptable. Celtic hospitality was such that the honored guest was offered the best of whatever the household had, even if it meant that the host would not eat that night.

Music and poetry are useful in establishing the atmosphere for your devotional rites and for focusing on your work. Modern Celtic music is evocative, but we don't really know what the music of the ancient Celts sounded like. Stay with something that sounds "Celtic" to you, but don't worry overmuch about the exact music you use. What is important is that it enables you to fall into a light trance state, where you can reach into the Otherworld to call out to the deities, Ancestors, or land spirits to come to your altar and receive your devotion.

You can also use poetry and music as offerings in your devotionals. These may be selections that you have chosen for the purpose, or compositions of your own making. The latter, even if they are not technically "perfect" or even particularly "good," are much more likely to be interesting and acceptable simply because they come from your own devotion and understanding of your relationships with the inhabitants of the Otherworld.

One very important point of a devotional is an attitude of listening and openness. We approach the Gods to grow into harmony with them, and to gain wisdom from associating with them. Information may not come during the actual time of your devotional. During the hours or days after each session, carefully observe the environment around you, watching for signs and symbols to manifest.

A final thought on dealing with deities is this: you may find yourself faced with choices of adoption by a deity or deific family, or service to them. They may impose *geasa*, or magical bindings, upon you. Taking on a *geas* is serious, as the tales show time and time again. Read the tales and know that if you take on a *geas*, you are responsible for its fulfillment even if it should cost your life. The tales show forcefully that violation of *geasa* is deadly business. Do not take it lightly. Ask questions and take time to meditate and consider before replying to any such offer. Fortunately, the Gods are patient. They are willing to wait for answers to these offers.

Remember that the Celts made contracts and took oaths that had force through many lifetimes. Accepting gifts and contact from the Gods may obligate you through this life and into the next. But that obligation does not have to be unpleasant. What the Gods desire most is our love and attendance.

The cautions given here should not produce the impression that the Gods are unreasonable. Their gifts are generously given and can take the form of great spiritual insight, wisdom, creative fertility and emotional strength. True gifts can be confirmed in the material realms. Information can be verified through research. Wisdom becomes manifest in dealings with other people. Strength and insight will become apparent through your actions.

Passing Through the Realms

Preparing the Journey

The Celts defined the world as made up of three different realms of reality, interconnected and interdependent. These are the realms of land, sea and sky. They are not merely the physical manifestations of earth, air and water, but are also the metaphysical realities, stretching into the Otherworld and underpinning the world we see, providing substance and support for our waking consciousness.

In the Celtic tales there are many different ways that people gain access to and knowledge of the Otherworld. Some of these seem specifically geared to journeying through particular realms. *Immram*, for instance, always refers to a voyage by water. This is the journey into the realm of sea.

Echtra is the "adventure" into the Sidhe mounds, and is the journey into the realm of land.

Aisling means "vision" or "dream." It is a process that brings an experience or an insight to a person, rather than carrying the person through a realm. It may be the process of "second sight" well known from Celtic folk tales and long family traditions. The tales give no examples of mortals journeying into the realm of sky, but there are many tales that show the Gods coming from there and revealing things. *Aisling*, therefore, will be the method we use to touch the sky.

So what is journeying, anyway? At its root, a journey is a method of getting into or seeing into an Otherworld place. Journeying requires acting consciously within a non-ordinary realm. This process can be accomplished in a number of different ways. A few simple methods are offered here. Work them with intention and with care. There are many methods that work, but each will produce somewhat different results and lead to different places. Know that journeying without a goal is really only aimless wandering, and to wander lost in the Otherworld is to invite madness. Be sure that you know what you want to achieve when you embark on your travels, for journeying is not without its dangers.

Consciousness is something we can define, in part at least, as being able to describe a tale in progress. By being conscious, we observe and classify the world, assigning it characters and a plot. Magic is the act of manipulating that story, telling a tale and starring in it, rather than simply observing it happening around us; we bring it to a conclusion that suits our goals. We consciously participate in creating our personal path. We call out our inner gift or inborn art, affirming it to the universe and expressing it. We become one with our magic and live it. This is the essence of the Celtic poem, the *Song of Aimirgen*, where the *fili* states "I am..."

The Otherworlds are not everywhere the same. There is no single Otherworld destination where all voyages arrive, nor are things the same there from season to season or moon to moon. In this respect, the Otherworld is much like our own world. Time moves differently there, and we must be aware of this as we journey. Our perceptions, and the perceptions of those who actually dwell in the Otherworld, influence each other. If we do not visit these shadow realms often enough, it seems that those who live there cannot "see" some places anymore. The mists between the worlds arise and the Wasteland grows, obscuring their view and ours.

Each time we journey we help to re-make the Otherworld landscape, aid in the task of healing the Wasteland, hold back the mists and re-define the boundaries of the three realms.

The Otherworld has a geography and a number of different "ecologies" just like our world does. Some regions are mountainous, others rolling heath or deeply forested, while still others are coastal or insular. Places *within* the mists are nearly formless and have little to orient on. Some places have little or no "real world" equivalent and must be dealt with entirely on their own terms.

When traveling in the Otherworld it helps to find landmarks and notable features to focus on so that you can begin to learn your way around. Particular entrances and gates lead to specific places. The same principle works in our world. If you purchase a plane ticket from New York to Boston, unless something goes terribly wrong you are unlikely to find yourself in Burbank. Keep your eyes open for signs that things might be shifting. You don't want to mistake the plane to Oakland for a plane to Aukland. Individual gates can shift somewhat, but they will lead to the same region or season even if they do not open into the same precise location each time.

If there is a sacred river, mound or other appropriate site in your area, it is worth a visit. Many of these places are useful as gateways into the Otherworlds. Take time before you journey to determine the "feel" of the place, for this will give you some indication of what you may find on the other side. Be sure to ask the permission and assistance of the land spirits that live there.

Know also that some Otherworld places are not active, so much as they hold "shadows" or "memories" of things that "have happened" in the past or the future. These "memories" are structured almost like a loop; they move through a set progression and reach a certain point, then begin again. The loop may take moments or subjective "months" to work through. Be aware that not all things that "have happened" are pleasant, and be alert to your emotional state while in these places and after returning from them. The quality of these locations feels somewhat different from other locales, but going to them can be very useful. One particular exercise that I have found helpful is to go looking for what I "did" on a project where I have hit a wall, and see how it "turned out" in the future. Ancient Celtic poetic invocations often lead to these places, bringing you to significant mythic events where you can observe the happenings.

When you journey, keep good notes about what you find and who you meet. They will become a resource for you, allowing you to map the things you find and to compare results with those who have been there before you as well. You are very likely to see things in a symbolic manner, rather than having a deity sit down for tea and a chat. The whole situation may be quite cryptic. Remember the symbols you see and the sequence of happenings. They can become important when you look back at your information later. These symbols can turn out to be things, places, even names of individuals. Be open to the information's arrival, but do not push to "see" something if there doesn't seem to be a flow.

In the tales, the divisions between what one finds on a particular kind of journey are small. It cannot be said, for instance, that one makes an *immram* strictly to find wisdom, but an *echtra* only for the purposes of finding an initiation. Wisdom, initiation, symbols and information are found in all the three realms. It is important to keep this in mind, for each of the realms supports the others as three legs support a stool. The focus of any particular journey may vary, but the result should be an increase in your understanding of what is happening in your life and in the world around you.

These journey techniques are self-directed meditations and visualizations. They begin with you, where you are now, and end with a return to normal waking consciousness. Each symbol in the Circle of Stones can be used to access a different realm, deity, or object. The symbolic Gates, in particular, are powerful openings into different Otherworld realms. Using the symbols of triskele, double spiral, Fionn's Window or the hole in the stone as the beginning of your meditation will allow a safe and very direct passage. The offered poetry and moving meditations are meant to create a sense of what each symbol means on one level or another. Think about these things as you ready yourself for your journey. The repeated poetry associated with each element of the circle acts as a sort of mantra to move the conscious mind toward a deeper state of awareness.

In preparing for a journey, you may wish to wear certain clothing set aside for ritual work, like a loose robe or non-restricting pants and a top. A meditational cloth was traditional in Celtic countries, to cover the head and reduce the distractions of light and movement. This practice probably goes back to the *fili* working divination wearing a yellow bull's hide. A hood or cloth acts as a sound baffle which amplifies chanting within the area around the head, enhancing the trance-inducing effect of sound. If you choose to use these things, use them only for ritual and journeying work, and not as your jogging togs or dress-up clothing. In setting these things apart from your everyday life, you cue yourself that you are moving into a special space and time when you don them.

An overwhelmingly clear characteristic of Celtic Otherworld access is that it is found only at a boundary between very different places or conditions. Doorways, river fords, bridges, gates, and of course the mists are the usual places that openings to the Otherworld are found. It is also marked by the appearance of unusual or out of place things.

Otherworld time does strange things. You may think you are journeying for only a few minutes, and return to find that hours have passes, or spend subjective hours in the Otherworld and find that you have journeyed but a few moments in "real" time. It is important to set aside at least an hour for your journey, and you may wish to set an alarm to alert you when this amount of "real world" time has passed, particularly if you have other things to do when you are done with your journeying. Another option is to have someone keep track of your time in the Otherworld for you.

The techniques offered here are *not* traditional for Celtic seers and mystics. Most of the traditional ways of gaining knowledge in Celtic tales involve madness, unconsciousness and the loss of control. Our society is not set up for having interactions with the sacred that resemble madness. Unless you have been trained by a Voudon practitioner, you are unlikely to have the necessary skills to interact with the sacred through loss of control to the deities. Instead, techniques are offered here which approach the content of the tales in a way that creates a safe interactive environment for gaining knowledge and for learning from and about the deities and the Otherworlds.

Guided meditation techniques appear in most cultures. There is nothing "shamanic" or unusual about individual or group trance states, whether they are induced by voice, lights, drumming, mind altering substances, placebo effect, or prolonged television watching. The determining factors are "set, setting, and dosage," as Timothy Leary explained in the 1960's. What is unusual in our culture is that we have to discuss the process at all. The repression of virtually all acceptable altered states, and the information acquired by their use, mandates taking a few precautionary steps.

Since these naturally occurring states are generally forbidden or ignored in our culture, a great deal of time is required to become familiar with the turf of one's own mind and body. This is where the journey begins, ends, and is interpreted. It may require dozens or even hundreds of sessions to learn how to relax and let go of expectations and the ordinary work-a-day mindset before proceeding on to useful journeying. A great deal of "noise" can be expected initially, until the mind stills and one can focus on the work at hand.

The first task is to choose an outdoor setting in the physical world that resembles the starting place of a journey in a tale. Depending on the type of voyage you wish to make, this may require a plain, a forested clearing, a sea shore, a wooden bridge across a stream, or a cave at the foot of a hill. An isolated site is usually best, to minimize disturbance. You will need to learn the site intimately, getting to know the smell of the earth, the feel of the sand under your feet, the texture of the rock you sit upon. After you have learned each of your chosen locations, you will not have to physically be present to begin your journeying, but until you can call up the site in perfect detail within your mind and hold it there, you will need to visit it regularly. For some people, a weekend visit to a particular stretch of beach may be enough. For others, a year of walking a well-worn pathway through the woods might be necessary to gain an intimate knowledge of the starting point.

If you have the luxury to do so, visit the site during several different times of day and night, and during every season. What trees and plants are there? What do they look like? What do they smell like? How do they feel? What animals and birds inhabit the area, and what do they eat? What stars can you see coming over the horizon? All these things are important. The Celts were certainly familiar with the places from which they began their journeys. For a shoreline site, get a tide chart and mark in your mind the high and low tide lines. Study the shells that you find on the beach, and watch for signs of sea mammals and other life.

Firmly associate the site with the realm you will be seeking. Meditate on the poetry and affirmations for the realm that are given in its section of the circle as you work in the area. The place must become a doorway for you, a gate into a different level of reality where the veils can be pierced.

The next step is to read Celtic adventure and journeying tales. A list of recommended reading is provided at the back of the book to give you a framework for your vision work. Locate photo books of Ireland, Scotland and Wales that show some of the actual sites of these events. Become intimately familiar with the tales and imagine yourself walking the lands that are described. Read the tales with a picture book at hand, and imagine how the places must have looked with hill-forts, deep forest, and massing warriors. Breathe the mystery of the *sidhe* mounds by examining pictures of sites like Brugh na Boyne (New Grange). Spend time trying to understand the mindset of the people who told and later wrote the tales. Absorb the love of description, the rich detail. The *sidhe* realms abound with light, mists, and jewel colors. Move slowly and do not expect everything to come to you all at once. Later you can take part in the tale as one of the actors rather than an observer, distanced from the action. Your final task will be to spin these tales for yourself, with you as the central character. As with all magical acts, your actions here will have consequences. Use common sense when confronted with unusual situations.

Building your voyage should incorporate three basic components: sound, motion, and emotion. Music, chanted poetry, spoken tales or the sounds of nature will all enhance the mood and setting of your journey and its beginning. One option is to take the poetry for the realm you travel into and repeat it with intent, gathering rhythm and psychic momentum, riding the words. Music that specifically creates a feeling of attachment to a realm can be played as a part of the process, either as prologue or as accompaniment for the actual travel. Working your journey within the physical realm you seek would provide you with the sounds of the natural world; singing leaves, waves lapping on shoreline. Listen for the inner voices.

With physical distractions at a minimum, the intention to journey gives rise to motion through the realms. The meditation cloth can be used to block out lights and shadows or to muffle or amplify sounds, allowing you to turn inward and open to the motion of inner travel. "Blindness" in the mundane world opens your eyes into the inner realms. Time and distance mutate and change within the context of your journey-tale. Mists rise and fall, and the scenery shifts. You walk, sail, fly. Gods and spirits move about you.

Identification with the tale links you emotionally to your voyage and to its results. The things you discover will have an emotional impact on your life outside your journey. Places will gain new meaning for you, not shared with others unless you choose to reveal them. You may find yourself dedicated to the service of a deity, or connecting with your ancestors. You may have strong emotional reactions to other actors you meet during your journeys. Some of these will be positive reactions. But do not be surprised if you meet figures that you dislike, or who dislike you. As it is in our world, so it is in the Otherworld as well.

It cannot be stressed highly enough that what you do in the Otherworld affects your life in the mundane world. You will find more than mere information awaits you. Your actions can be transformative, in both positive and negative ways. Act with care, and be prepared to see your outer life shift and move with the magical acts in which you participate as you travel the Otherworld realms.

Making the Journey

The first step is to choose the realm in which you will seek information. The format of your journey and mythic tales will be different for each realm. Think about the nature of your quest, and what you ultimately wish to find. Consider which realm you are most likely to find your answers in, based upon your readings of the tales. Your degree of success will depend in large part upon your preparations, so do not feel compelled to rush simply because the process of preparation may be somewhat less interesting than the actual journey itself.

Landmarks will be most easily found in the realm of land. It is recommended that you start with *echtrai* this realm in order to become familiar with the techniques and the process. *Immrama* through the realm of sea are marked most often by lack of easily discernable landmarks, but this can be overcome once you are used to the state and familiar with the process of journeying. *Aisling* come in sleep and deliberately induced visionary states, but the dream reality can be filled with material that is very easily misinterpreted, and can also give rise to much self-deception. The realm of sky should be saved for when you have a great deal of experience. The sample journey structure will presume that you are beginning an *echtra*.

Although it is not particularly traditional, a ritual bath is recommended before you begin your journey, as purification and preparation for your work. Along with the removal of symbolic impurity, the bath will relax you and begin to put you into an appropriate state for exploring the Otherworld. Relaxation is a necessary element for effective journeying. Remember also that water is a boundary between "normal" reality and the Otherworld places you wish to visit. The bath symbolizes your crossing from this world into the liminal space between worlds where the Otherworld gates are accessed. You can use plain water, or a bath oil or bath salt having a pleasant scent that you associate with the land. Woody or earthy herbal scents work well.

There is little evidence for the use of ritual oils or incenses among the Celts before the introduction of Christian ritual, and so their use and symbolism need not have "traditional" meanings in Celtic culture. Anything that you find appropriate for reasons of scent or magical correspondence will be acceptable. Failing a full bath, add your scented oils or salts to a large bowl of water and bathe your face and hands, knowing that you are participating in the symbolic crossing of a boundary.

You should go physically to the place you have chosen to represent your entry point for the realm of land. If this is not possible, then create the realm in your physical space as much as you are able. In the last analysis, your mind is the only tool you really need, but props of all kinds can be most helpful. For your first journeys, you will want as many props to assist you as you can gather, and being at your site physically is one of the best ways to connect with your chosen realm. You will have less need of these cues later.

You will want to wear loose clothing, including a meditation cloth the size of a large square scarf or a small blanket. It should be of a dark color, patterned with a tartan if you like, that will obscure the light and distractions. If you are going on your voyage outside, take someone with you to act as a "spotter" in case of possible disturbances from environmental causes, or from chance passers-by. If you must be indoors, then make sure you are in a place where you will be undisturbed by ringing phones, blaring radios or televisions, and family members or housemates, at least as much as possible. Low lighting will also help to cut the distractions to a minimum.

Close your eyes and cover your head with your meditation cloth. Closing your eyes here is preparation for opening them into the Otherworld.

Begin a recitation of the daily round, as you would if you were preparing for sleep. Volume is not necessary, or even desirable. What is important is that you can continue the chanting for an extended period of time. Breathe in an appropriate rhythm that allows you to flow with the poetry and still take a good breath. See yourself clearly at the various points in the meditation series. As you recite the poetry for the Inner Flame, you should begin a Cauldron meditation, described below. Observe carefully as you light the inner watchfires.

Take a few minutes to breathe slowly in and out, to a very slow count of three. Inhale on a three count, hold for a three count, and exhale on a three count, then begin again. Do not rush. There is no need to set a speed record, or to cause hyperventilation. Concentrate the energies of your breath first in your lower abdomen, in the pelvic girdle, with a series of nine breaths. Fill your lower abdomen with warmth. This is your Cauldron of Warming. It connects you with the forces of physical life. This cauldron is active in all people.

Continue the cycle with a second series of nine three count breaths. You are filling your chest with warmth and energy as you continue to hold the energy within your abdomen. This is your Cauldron of Motion. It creates the motion within you that propels you on your journey. This cauldron traditionally requires work to activate, but may be partially active in some people. It may activate at times of initiation or crisis.

The third series of nine three count breaths fills your head while maintaining the warmth and energy of the previous two cauldrons. This is your Cauldron of Wisdom. It helps you to perceive, comprehend and interpret the information you receive while you travel in the Otherworld. This cauldron requires training and many years of hard work to activate fully, if it activates at all. In Irish tradition, its full activation is the sign of divine inspiration, and will transform your life. Only *filidh* of the highest rank attained the activation of this cauldron.

Proceed through the poetry of the strand until you reach the poem for Sacred Land. Instead of nine repetitions of the poetry, one for each bead, repeat the poem until you achieve a rhythm and a sense of movement. When you get to this point, continue chanting the poem and begin to create your starting point within your head. Sense it in every detail. Be aware of the scents in the air, the temperature, the movement around you. Place yourself into the scene and identify with it strongly. Note the weather, the season, the time of day or night. If the stars or moon are in sight, note the phase of the moon and any recognizable constellations. Your journeying persona should be clothed appropriately for the time and the place. You may be riding a fine steed, or pursuing a stag through the forest. Perhaps you are walking a well-worn path across the heath. Continue your chant and let the tale take you.

Follow your tale, observing carefully. Watch for unusual animal life. Observe gateways and remember the paths you take. With luck, you will eventually come to the mists. They will probably arise suddenly, obscuring your view of the landscape around you. Disorientation may set in. This is to be expected and is not a problem. You may be "lost" but you can *always* find your way out of the mists back into the mundane world. When the mists engulf you, spend some time there before you proceed, getting a feel for the between spaces. You will probably spend a lot of time in the mists over the years. The Irish considered the mist to be "the Cloak of Manannan." You may not see him, but he is always present in the mists.

It is extremely unlikely that you will meet the Gods on your first journeys. In fact, it may take you months of journeying before you are even able to pass through the mists. This is a long term project, so be prepared to spend a good deal of time working through your tales. Listen to your instincts regarding whether you should speak or be silent when at last you meet another character in your tale. Note things said to you, and who said them.

Remember symbols that are shown to you or that seem to stand out for any reason. Things that appear in threes or nines are very important. Every tiny detail may be meaningful, so do not ignore little things.

One thing you may meet in your early journeys are your own projections. You will naturally expect to meet with unusual things and people. Be prepared to meet things that you have created in your own mind. It will take time and practice to tell these things from the real inhabitants of the Otherworld realms. A good clue that you have met a projection is finding an individual who offers to reveal all the mysteries to you right away. Always check the information you get with reading, research and practice when you return, to weed out the elements of self-deception.

Be content when you meet with the local land spirits, or the shades of the ancestors. They are wise and can teach you, perhaps better at first than a deity. You will have an easier time understanding the ancestors, because they have lived as you have, and they speak in terms that humans comprehend. They are usually but not always friendly. Treat them with great respect, for you will one day join them here. The ancestors can introduce you to land spirits and deities.

Land spirits have things to share as well, but they may act as tricksters. This is not because they dislike you, but because they have a different sense of time and values than humans do. Deal with them carefully and examine all the angles of any offers they make to you before you accept or decline. Be prepared to live with the consequences of any decisions you make, for good or ill. Actions in the Otherworld can have great impact in your mundane life. Land spirits may also introduce you to deities, but this will usually arise in a situation that is mutually beneficial.

Meeting the deities is a thing you may wait a long time to accomplish. Remember that a thing is only worth the effort you have expended on it. The deities have deep lessons to teach, and they can demand a great deal from you in return. Accepting the offer of a deity can have lifelong repercussions. They may give you gifts, or they may test you. They might show you fragments of a dream and expect you to know what they mean by it. Communication is not likely to take place in words, at least at first. Realize that their communication can be very cryptic. Deities can also act as tricksters. Consider all your actions around the deities very carefully and know that you will be judged according to your actions and reactions.

Deities may introduce you to the rest of their family, or to others with whom they have contractual or social relationships. Remember that Celtic deities are affiliated with each other in lines of friendship and rivalry. Be alert to emotional tones around you, and watch for clues in the actions of your hosts. Taking the time to learn Celtic codes of behavior as expressed in the tales can only help you in these situations.

At some point, it will be time for you to return from your journey. You may simply decide that you have spent enough time wandering in the mists for one day. Your travel partner may have notified you of your time limit for the session. Perhaps you have found something interesting that you want to spend some time thinking about before you proceed further. It may also happen that you will be summarily dismissed by some actor in your tale and that no further journeying is possible at this point. Or you might even find the goal of your particular journey. Whatever the circumstance, it is time to return to waking consciousness.

If you have reached beyond the mists in your travels, you should retrace your path as much as possible until you return to the mists. From the mists, you can bring yourself home. Continue chanting the poetry for Sacred Land and begin to focus on the words instead of the motion of your travel process, returning to the starting point of your journey. When you attain an acute awareness of the actual words and rhythm of your chanting and your breathing, move to the next poem in the string. Continue the string counterclockwise and proceed as though you were working through your normal circle recitation, returning gradually to a waking state as you go. Once again, there is no rush, no reason to hurry.

Upon reaching the Inner Flame, reverse the Cauldron meditation, moving down from the head to the abdomen. Bring your awareness through to the mundane world and refocus on the physical environment around you. Ending with the Gate of Divine Mysteries, reaffirm your self and your identity, and end the inner phase of the work.

When you have returned, take some time to reconnect with the physical world. Bathe hands and face in the waters of your ritual bath, to symbolize crossing back into the mundane world. Gather your materials together and put them all away, then sit down for a cup of tea or a small snack. If you have a working partner for the process, discuss your journey and your findings with them. Keeping a journey log for your notes and analysis is very useful, and you can record your information at this time, while it is still fresh in your mind. Draw symbols that you were shown, note conversations you had, sketch maps of the places you have seen and routes taken. Record your impressions with as much emotional tone and vividness as possible, keeping track of the season or time, the colors of things, anything that seems at all important.

The evaluation process is just as important as the journey itself. It is through analysis of what you have seen and experienced that you learn and grow. This enables you to go further in each journey. With each additional journey you make, you gather information that allows you to ask the right questions, and these questions in turn allow you to get answers that help you on your path. Continual reading of the Celtic tales and other works gives you context for the interpretation of your experiences. The process of analysis and reading also helps you to sort the wheat from the chaff, separating the useful material from the projections and the self-deceptive interpretations. If a thing is jarringly out of place, or simply does not quite fit the context, examine it closely and be sure it should be there. This may be a clue that the information is not good. If you determine that it does belong despite the fact that it seems out of place, you will need to figure out why it belongs, and also why it appears to be out of place. Both of these things will provide information.

Remember that none of this material exists alone. Everything in the universe is connected to everything else in some way. Celtic cultures provide a number of specific contexts to show when material is important and some very precise symbols which indicate how things are important. If things are confusing, set them aside for a time and wait. Eventually the mysteries become clear.

The techniques offered here are only a sample of what can be done with a little imagination and determination. Your Circle of Stones can be a powerful tool for exploring the Otherworlds and meeting the Gods on their own ground. The gate is open. It is time to step through.

Notes

1. Rees, Alwyn & Brinley, *Celtic Heritage, Ancient Tradition in Ireland and Wales*, Thames & Hudson, New York 1990, p 122.

2. MacAlister, R.A. Stewart, *Lebor Gabala Erenn: The Book of the Taking of Ireland, part IV*, Irish Texts Society volume XLI, Dublin 1941, p 107.

3. The English translations of the poetry are based on those listed in the noted source material, however they are largely my own.

4. Irish source: *Do Ghabhalaibh Erend*. No publication data was available in the edition used for this work.

5. This pillar is not the equivalent of the Qabalistic Middle Pillar. Instead it is a world tree, like those found in the mythology of most cultures.

6. The internal cauldrons are similar to, but not the same as the energy chakras of Indian yoga. They were probably located in the abdomen, chest and head. Early Irish poets were said to have activated and used the cauldrons as they became more proficient in the arts of poetry, divination and magic.

7. This piece is an original work composed for this book.

8. Irish source: Murphy, Gerard, *Early Irish Lyrics, Eighth to Twelfth Century*, Clarendon Press, Oxford 1956. From the eighth century poem "The Lament of the Old Woman of Beare."

9. Scottish Gaelic source: Carmichael, Alexander, *Carmina Gadelica*, vol II, Scottish Academic Press, Edinburgh 1972.

10. Scottish Gaelic source: Carmichael, Alexander, *Carmina Gadelica*, vol II, Scottish Academic Press, Edinburgh 1972.

11. Irish source: *Do Ghabhalaibh Eren*. No publication data was available in the edition used for this work.

12. Irish source: MacAlister, R.A.S., *Lebor Gabala Erenn part V*, Irish Texts Society vol XLIV.

13. Scottish Gaelic source: Carmichael, Alexander, *Carmina Gadelica*, vol II, Scottish Academic Press, Edinburgh 1972.

14. Scottish Gaelic source: Carmichael, Alexander, *Carmina Gadelica*, vol I, Scottish Academic Press, Edinburgh 1972. Original reference was to the Archangel Michael.

15. Scottish Gaelic source: Carmichael, Alexander, *Carmina Gadelica*, vol III, Scottish Academic Press, Edinburgh 1972.

16. Scottish Gaelic source: Carmichael, Alexander, *Carmina Gadelica*, vol II, Scottish Academic Press, Edinburgh 1972.

17. Scottish Gaelic source: Carmichael, Alexander, *Carmina Gadelica*, vol I, Scottish Academic Press, Edinburgh 1972. The first line originally read "a knife keen..."

18. Scottish Gaelic source: Carmichael, Alexander, *Carmina Gadelica*, vol II, Scottish Academic Press, Edinburgh 1972. Originally part of a spell for healing the color used was changed by this author from red (a reference to blood) to green.

19. Scottish Gaelic source: Carmichael, Alexander, *Carmina Gadelica*, vol II, Scottish Academic Press, Edinburgh 1972.

20. Irish source: Breatnach, Liam, *The Cauldron of Poesy, Eriu #32*, pp 45-93, 1981.

21. Irish source: O'Curry, Eugene, *Lectures on the Manuscript Materials of Ancient Irish History*,1878.

22. Irish source: Murphy, Gerard, *Early Irish Lyrics, Eighth to Twelfth Century*, Clarendon Press, Oxford 1956. From the eighth century poem "The Lament of the Old Woman of Beare."

23. This piece is an original work composed for this book.

24. Irish source: *Do Ghabhalaibh Erend*. No publication data was available in the edition used for this work.

Pronunciation Guide

This is intended as a rough guide to pronouncing Old Irish. No one actually speaks the language now, so even the scholars are making a guess at it. The stress in a word usually falls in the first syllable.

b: (beginning a word) boy (middle or end of a word) v or w as in never or win.
c or cc: (beginning a word) candle. It is never pronounced as an s. In the middle or at the end of a word it is a g, as in egg.
d: (beginning a word) dog (middle or end of a word) th as in that.
f: fire
g: girl
h: hill
l, ll: lame
m, mb, mm: (beginning a word) mow, (middle or end of a word) v or w as in never or win.
n, nd, nn: name
p: (beginning a word) post, (middle or end of a word) b as in boy.
r, rr: rolled as in Spanish *serrano*.
s, ss: (before a, o or u, or after a, o or u at the end of a word) silly (before e or i, or after e or i at the end of a word) ship.
t, tt: (beginning a word) toe, (middle or end of a word) th as in thick.
a, ai: father or law
ae, ai: aisle
e, ei, eo, eoi: test
i: tin
i, iu, iui: teem
o, oi: rot or tone
oe, oi: oil
u, ui: put or moon
ua, uai: poor

Glossary

Aisling: Dream, vision. Received inspiration from the realm of Endless Sky.

Beltain: The Celtic spring festival. The name means "bright fire."

Bile: The God of death and the ancestors. Husband of Danu, and ancestor of Gods and mortals. A sacred tree.

Boann: The Goddess of the Boyne river and of cattle. She guards the Well of Wisdom in the Otherworld.

Coire Ansic: The un-dry cauldron, the Cauldron of Daghda. This was the ever-full cauldron of plenty.

Daghda: The "Good God" of the Irish. God of magic and druidry. Called the "All-Father."

Danu: The Celtic "Great Mother" Goddess. She is the primal European Goddess of rivers.

Duile: "Elements," created things, nature, creation.

Echtra: Adventure. A journey through the realm of Sacred Land. Plural form is Echtrai.

Fili: An Irish sacred or ritual poet. Plural form is filidh.

Eponymous: "Name-giving," one who gives their name to something.

Fionn's Window: An ogham glyph consisting of five concentric circles which have the ogham letters arranged around them. Found in the Book of Ballymote, a 14th century Irish manuscript.

Geas: A form of ritual binding found in many Irish tales.

House of Donn: The Otherworld place where the spirits of the dead go.

Imbas: Sacred inspiration, poetic frenzy. It was envisioned as fire arising from the Well of Wisdom.

Immram: Sea voyage. A journey through the realm of Eternal Sea. Plural form is Immrama.

Lia Fail: The Stone of Fal. One of the four great treasures of the Tuatha de Danann.

Liminal: At the edge, boundary or border of something. A place in between two states or places.

Lugh: The God of crafts and arts. Champion and war-leader of the Tuatha de Danann.

Manannan: The Celtic God of the sea, mists and journeys.

Nuadha: King of the Tuatha de Danann. A manifestation of the wounded king, his arm was lost in battle and replaced with a silver arm.

Ogham: An Irish alphabet.

Samhain: The Celtic feast of the new year. A time of remembering the ancestors. The name means "summer's end."

Taliesin: A Welsh bard and magician.

Triskele: A triple spiral. This motif is found throughout the Celtic world and originates in the neolithic era.

Bibliography & Further Reading

Breatnach, Liam, *The Cauldron of Poesy*, Eriu #32, pp 45-93, 1981

Carmichael, Alexander, *Carmina Gadelica*, Lindisfarne Press 1990

Chadwick, Nora, *The Celts*, Penguin, Middlesex 1985

Cross, Tom Peete and Clark Harris Slover, *Ancient Irish Tales*, Barnes & Noble, Totowa NJ 1988

Cunliffe, Barry, *The Celtic World : An Illustrated History of the Celtic Race, Their Culture, Customs and Legends*, Greenwich House, NY 1986

Dames, Michael, *Mythic Ireland*, Thames & Hudson, New York 1992

Davidson, HR Ellis, *Myths and Symbols in Pagan Europe: Early Scandinavian and Celtic Religions*, Syracuse University Press, Syracuse 1988

Dillon, Myles, *Early Irish Literature*, University of Chicago Press, Chicago 1948

Ellis, Peter Berresford, *A Dictionary of Irish Mythology*, Oxford University Press, Oxford 1987

Evans-Wentz, WY, *The Fairy Faith in Celtic Countries*, Citadel Press, NY 1990

Gantz, Jeffrey, *Early Irish Myths and Sagas*, Penguin, London 1988

Gray, Elizabeth A, ed. *Cath Maige Tuired: The Second Battle of Mag Tuired*, Irish Texts Society, vol LIV, Leinster 1982

Green, Miranda, *Symbol & Image in Celtic Religious Art*, Routledge, New York 1992

Henry, PL, *The Cauldron of Poesy*, Studia Celtica #14/15, pp 114-128 1979/1980

Jackson, Kenneth Hurlstone, *The Oldest Irish Tradition: A Window on the Iron Age*, Cambridge University Press, Cambridge 1964

Jackson, Kenneth Hurlstone ed. *A Celtic Miscellany*, Penguin, NY 1971

Kinsella, Thomas, *The Tain*, University of Philadelphia Press, Philadelphia 1985

Littleton, C. Scott, *The New Comparative Mythology: An Anthropological Assessment of the Theories of Georges Dumezil*, 3ed, University of California Press, Berkeley 1982

MacAlister, R.A. Stewart, *Lebor Gabala Erenn: The Book of the Taking of Ireland, part IV*, Irish Texts Society volume XLI, Dublin 1941

MacCana, Proinsias, *Celtic Mythology*, Hamlyn, London 1970

Mallory, J. P., *In Search of the Indo-Europeans*, Thames & Hudson, NY 1989

Murphy, Gerard, *Early Irish Lyrics, Eighth to Twelfth Century*, Clarendon Press, Oxford 1956